20 FUN FACTS ABOUT TENOCHTITLÁN

BY EMILY MAHONEY

Gareth Stevens
PUBLISHING

Please visit our website, www.garethstevens.com. For a free color catalog of all our high-quality books, call toll free 1-800-542-2595 or fax 1-877-542-2596.

Cataloging-in-Publication Data

Names: Mahoney, Emily.
Title: 20 fun facts about Tenochtitlan / Emily Mahoney.
Description: New York : Gareth Stevens Publishing, 2020. | Series: Fun fact file: world wonders! | Includes glossary and index.
Identifiers: ISBN 9781538237625 (pbk.) | ISBN 9781538237649 (library bound) | ISBN 9781538237632 (6 pack)
Subjects: LCSH: Aztecs–History–Juvenile literature. | Mexico–History–Conquest, 1519-1540–Juvenile literature. | Templo Mayor (Mexico City, Mexico) – Juvenile literature.
Classification: LCC F1219.73 M32 2019 | DDC 972'.018–dc23

First Edition

Published in 2020 by
Gareth Stevens Publishing
111 East 14th Street, Suite 349
New York, NY 10003

Copyright © 2020 Gareth Stevens Publishing

Designer: Sarah Liddell
Editor: Kristen Nelson

Photo credits: Cover, p. 1 (main) DEA PICTURE LIBRARY/Contributor/De Agostini/ Getty Images; file folder used throughout David Smart/Shutterstock.com; binder clip used throughout luckyraccoon/Shutterstock.com; wood grain background used throughout ARENA Creative/Shutterstock.com; p. 5 Diego Grandi/Shutterstock.com; p. 6 Kgv88/ Wikimedia Commons; p. 7 Lepusinensis/Shutterstock.com; p. 8 API/Contributor/ Gamma-Rapho/Getty Images; p. 9 WitR/Shutterstock.com; p. 10 Joseph Sorrentino/ Shutterstock.com; p. 11 Grafissimo/DigitalVision Vectors/Getty images; p. 12 Nastasic/ DigitalVision Vectors/Getty Images; p. 13 ZU_09/DigitalVision Vectors/Getty Images; p. 14 DEA/G. DAGLI ORTI/De Agostini Picture Library/Getty Images; p. 16 Ptcamn~commonswiki/Wikimedia Commons; p. 17 Joyborg/Wikimedia Commons; p. 18 Luis Dafos/Moment/Getty Images; p. 19 DEA PICTURE LIBRARY/Contributor/De Agostini/Getty Images; p. 20 Georgios Kollidas/Shutterstock.com; pp. 21, 22 Print Collector/ Contributor/Hulton Archive/Getty Images; p. 23 Getty Images/Handout/Archive Photos/ Getty Images; p. 24 UniversalImagesGroup/Contributor/Universal Images Group/ Getty Images; p. 25 steve estvanik/Shutterstock.com; p. 26 Anadolu Agency/Contributor/ Anadolu Agency/Getty Images; p. 29 DEA/G. DAGLI ORTI/Contributor/De Agostini/ Getty Images.

Printed in the United States of America

CPSIA compliance information: Batch #CS19GS: For further information contact Gareth Stevens, New York, New York at 1-800-542-2595.

CONTENTS

Words in the glossary appear in **bold** type the first time they are used in the text.

WONDER OF THE PAST

Tenochtitlán (TEH-noch-tiht-LAHN) was the capital city of the Aztec **civilization**. The Aztecs had a large empire in central and southern Mexico in the 1400s and early 1500s. It was a grand capital that showed off their wealth and power.

Tenochtitlán was advanced for its time. This could especially be seen in what the Aztecs built in their city as it grew. Today, we know many surprising and interesting facts about the city's history. The first is that it existed for less than 200 years!

While it's in ruin today, Tenochtitlán was once a beautiful and large city filled with people.

THE AMAZING AZTECS

TENOCHTITLÁN WAS FOUNDED ALMOST 700 YEARS AGO!

The Aztecs founded Tenochtitlán in 1325. Before they settled there, the Aztecs were **nomads** from the north who often fought other groups in central Mexico as they moved around. They were likely hunters and gatherers.

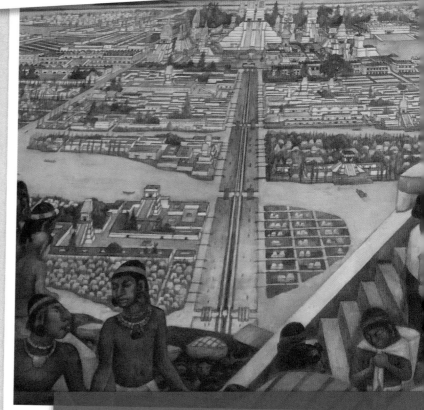

Tenochtitlán was named after an Aztec ruler named Tenoch.

A picture of the story of the founding of Tenochtitlán is on the Mexican flag. In another telling of this story, the god says to look for a prickly pear cactus and build a temple there.

AN AZTEC STORY SAYS FOUNDERS LOOKED FOR A SIGN FOR WHERE TO BUILD THEIR CITY.

One of the Aztec gods told ruler Tenoch in a **vision** that the place where he saw an eagle sitting on a cactus eating a snake was where he should build the great Aztec city.

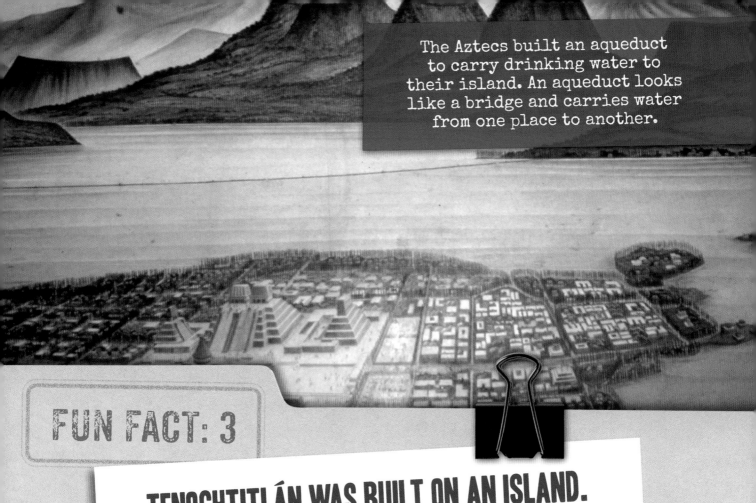

The Aztecs built an aqueduct to carry drinking water to their island. An aqueduct looks like a bridge and carries water from one place to another.

FUN FACT: 3

TENOCHTITLÁN WAS BUILT ON AN ISLAND.

It started as a small village near the western shore of Lake Texcoco in present-day Mexico City, Mexico. By the late 1400s, it was becoming a well-planned city laid out in a grid. Temples and government buildings were found at the city's center.

TOGETHER, TENOCHTITLÁN AND TLATELOLCO WERE ABOUT FOUR TIMES THE SIZE OF CENTRAL PARK IN NEW YORK CITY.

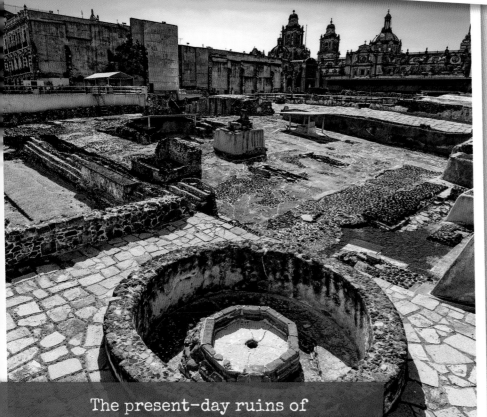

The present-day ruins of Tenochtitlán can help to give you an idea of how big the city once was.

The Aztec city of Tlatelolco was founded to the north of Tenochtitlán. Their combined size was about 5.4 square miles (14 sq km).

LIFE IN TENOCHTITLÁN

THE AZTECS FARMED IN THE SWAMPS AROUND TENOCHTITLÁN.

The Aztecs didn't have good farmland on their island. Instead, they built *chinampas*, or man-made islands, on which to farm. *Chinampas* were made of mud and dead plants brought up from the bottom of the lake. Farmers even lived in huts on these islands!

Today, chinampas are sometimes simply called floating gardens.

PEOPLE LIVING IN TENOCHTITLÁN HAD A CURFEW.

A warning using either drums or a large conch shell was given around sunset to signal the end of the working day. Everyone had to be inside a few hours later. This made it easier to keep the city safe at night.

PEOPLE USED CANOES TO GET AROUND THE CITY OF TENOCHTITLÁN.

As many as 200,000 canoes may have been in use on Lake Texcoco in the early 1500s. The Aztecs used canoes to travel off the island. They also built **canals** across the island that allowed them to travel throughout the city of Tenochtitlán.

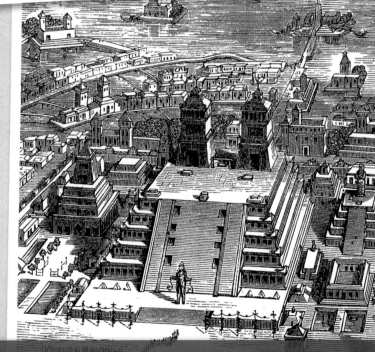

The Aztecs could also cross the swampy water around the island to reach the mainland by using causeways they built. Causeways are low roads built across wet ground.

CITIZENS OF TENOCHTITLÁN DIDN'T SHOP WITH MONEY!

They still went to the market to get food and goods such as cloth, thread, gemstones, and gold. But, they bartered, or traded what they had, for the items they needed. In large towns within the city, markets were set up every day.

NOT EVERYONE IN TENOCHTITLÁN COULD HAVE A HOUSE WITH A SECOND STORY.

Because of the class system in the city and Aztec **culture**, the upper classes could sometimes have homes with two floors. Farmers and other commoners couldn't! Certain clothes could only be worn by the upper classes, too.

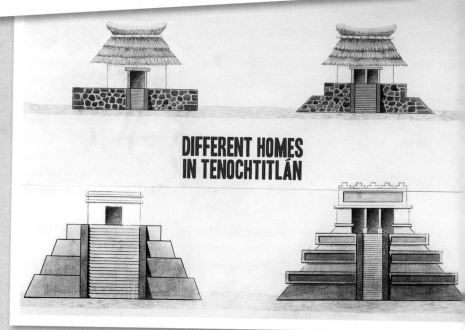

DIFFERENT HOMES IN TENOCHTITLÁN

RULER AND HIS FAMILY

NOBLES
(GOVERNMENT OFFICIALS, PRIESTS, MILITARY LEADERS)

COMMONERS
(TRADERS, CRAFTSPEOPLE, FARMERS, FISHERS, LABORERS)

PEASANTS

SLAVES

In Aztec **society,** it was possible to move up in social class. Even slaves could earn their freedom through work!

FUN FACT: 10

THE TEMPLO MAYOR WAS LOCATED IN THE CENTER OF TENOCHTITLÁN.

The pyramid of the Templo Mayor, or "great temple," was the largest building in Tenochtitlán. It was in the center of the city. That makes sense since the Aztec people believed that **worship** of their gods should be central to their lives.

The Templo Mayor wasn't uncovered until 1978! First, workers found this stone. Soon after, the buried temple was discovered.

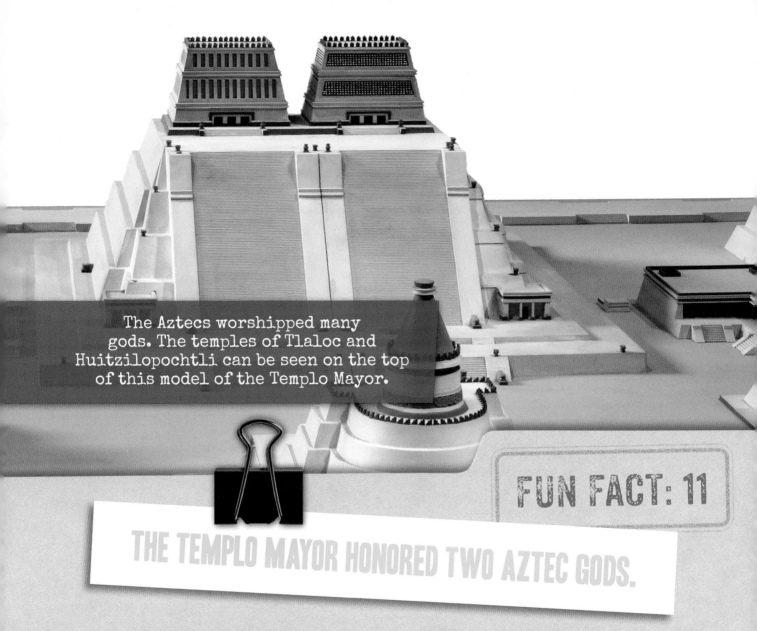

The Aztecs worshipped many gods. The temples of Tlaloc and Huitzilopochtli can be seen on the top of this model of the Templo Mayor.

THE TEMPLO MAYOR HONORED TWO AZTEC GODS.

Tlaloc was the god of rain, and Huitzilopochtli was the god of war and the sun. The Aztecs built a temple for each of these gods at the top of the pyramid.

Parts of the Templo Mayor are still standing today.

ALL OF THE TEMPLO MAYOR WAS BUILT BY HAND.

Its construction began with Tenochtitlán's founding. It was rebuilt and added to several times by different rulers. Each piece had to be moved and placed by a person! At its tallest, it was about the height of two and a half telephone poles, or about 90 feet (27.4 m).

HUMAN SACRIFICES TOOK PLACE AT THE TEMPLO MAYOR.

Sacrifices were part of Aztec culture and beliefs.

In the late 1400s, a new ruler rebuilt the outermost part of the temple. At the reopening celebration, thousands of prisoners were sacrificed to the Aztec gods. The sacrifices were meant to help keep the gods happy.

19

SPANISH INVASION

AT FIRST, SPANISH CONQUISTADORS WERE WELCOMED INTO TENOCHTITLÁN.

A conquistador named Hernán Cortés and his men sailed from Spain to current-day Mexico to explore the area and claim land for Spain. The first natives they met gave them presents, including slaves!

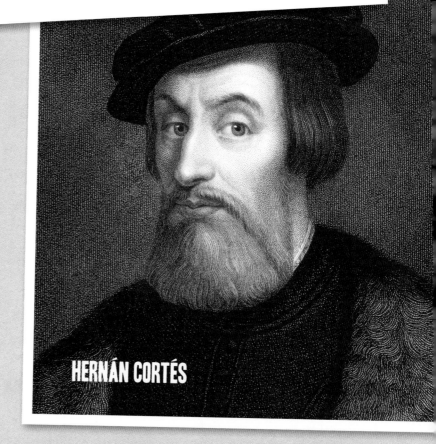

HERNÁN CORTÉS

When Cortés first entered Tenochtitlán in 1519, the ruler was Montezuma II. However, Cortés captured Montezuma and gained power in the city through him.

CORTÉS NEEDED A TRANSLATOR TO SPEAK TO THE AZTECS.

Cortés spoke Spanish, which the Aztecs didn't understand. He spoke Spanish to someone who translated his words into Mayan, and then another person translated the Mayan words into Nahuatl, the language of the Aztecs.

21

MILLIONS OF AZTECS WERE KILLED BY SPANISH DISEASES.

The Aztecs in Tenochtitlán fought back against the Spanish taking over their city. But in 1520, a new disease, or illness, called smallpox spread through

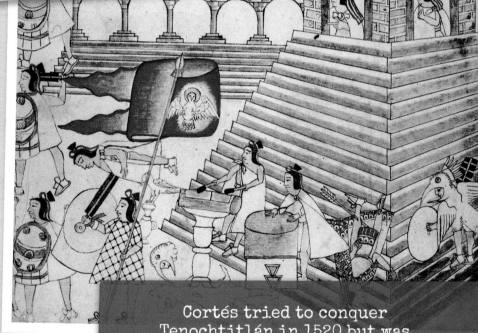

Cortés tried to conquer Tenochtitlán in 1520 but was pushed out by Aztec fighters.

the population of Tenochtitlán and into the empire beyond.

The many deaths it caused made the Aztecs weaker.

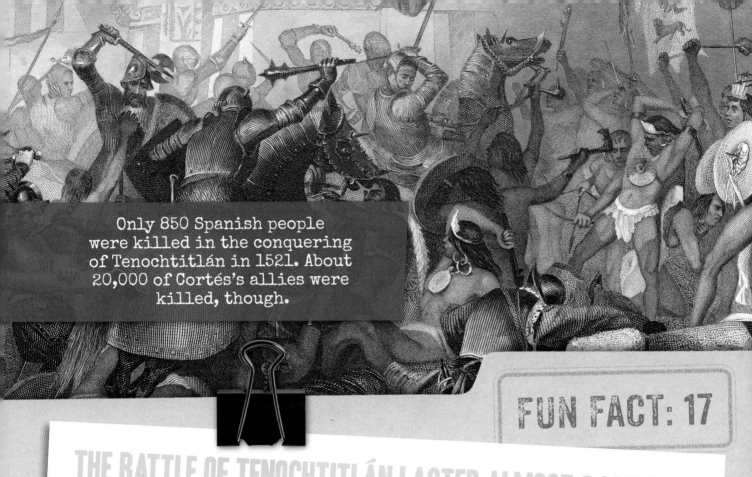

Only 850 Spanish people were killed in the conquering of Tenochtitlán in 1521. About 20,000 of Cortés's allies were killed, though.

THE BATTLE OF TENOCHTITLÁN LASTED ALMOST 3 MONTHS.

Cortés became allies, or friends, with other groups of native people in present-day Mexico. These allies helped his army overthrow the Aztecs at Tenochtitlán. Cortés's army blocked off the main ways on and off the island. About 240,000 Aztecs were killed in the fighting.

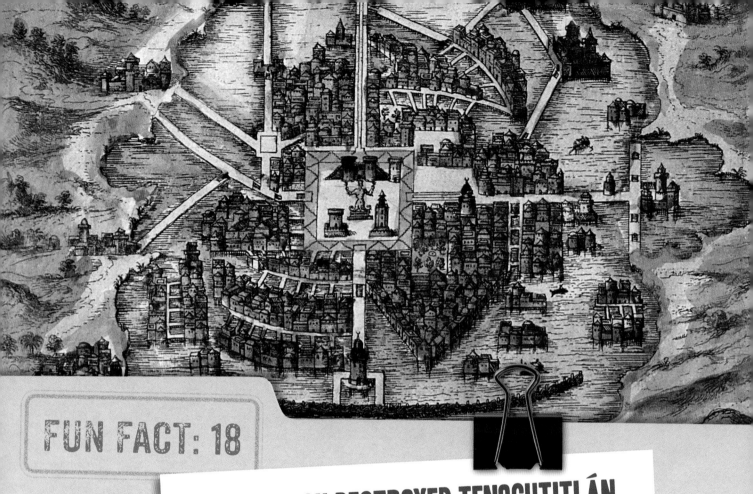

THE SPANISH DESTROYED TENOCHTITLÁN.

On top of the ruins, they built Mexico City. The Spanish now ruled what had been the Aztec Empire and more of modern-day Mexico. They called it New Spain. Cortés was put in charge for a time by the Spanish king, Charles I.

TENOCHTITLÁN TODAY

YOU CAN TAKE A BOAT ON THE CANALS BUILT NEAR WHERE TENOCHTITLÁN ONCE STOOD.

Many canals were built during the time of the Aztecs, but few remain in Mexico today.

To see what's left of what was once one of the largest cities in the world, you have to travel to Mexico City. There, you can take a brightly colored boat to see the floating gardens along the water.

25

DESCENDANTS OF AZTECS WHO LIVED IN TENOCHTITLÁN STILL LIVE IN MEXICO TODAY.

About 1 million people in Mexico still speak the Nahuatl language of the Aztecs. These descendants still live in towns and villages in central Mexico, near where their ancestors settled.

There's still a lot to learn about Tenochtitlán and the Aztecs who lived there! These skulls were found near the Templo Mayor in 2017.

TIMELINE OF TENOCHTITLÁN

1325
TENOCHTITLÁN IS FOUNDED.

1487
ONE RULER'S CONSTRUCTION ON THE TEMPLO MAYOR IS FINISHED, AND MANY PRISONERS ARE SACRIFICED AT THE CELEBRATION.

1502
THE MOST FAMOUS AZTEC KING, MONTEZUMA II, BEGINS HIS RULE OF TENOCHTITLÁN.

MARCH 4, 1519
HERNÁN CORTÉS LANDS IN PRESENT-DAY MEXICO.

NOVEMBER 8, 1519
CORTÉS ARRIVES IN TENOCHTITLÁN.

1520
THE SPANISH BEGIN THEIR TAKEOVER OF TENOCHTITLÁN. MONTEZUMA II DIES.

MAY 22, 1521
THE BATTLE OF TENOCHTITLÁN BEGINS.

AUGUST 13, 1521
TENOCHTITLÁN FALLS TO CORTÉS AND THE CITY IS DESTROYED.

1522
THE SPANISH REBUILD TENOCHTITLÁN AND CALL IT MEXICO CITY, CAPITAL OF NEW SPAIN.

A SHORT TIME

Although the city of Tenochtitlán only existed for about 200 years, it's remembered as one of the most advanced civilizations of its time. The Aztecs found creative ways to farm and build a well-planned city as well as canals and causeways.

We can use what's left of Tenochtitlán to piece together the history of this grand Aztec civilization. What would the Aztecs have been able to accomplish if the Spanish hadn't invaded their great city?

AZTEC STONE OF THE SUN

Artifacts are things made by people in the past. Today, we study the artifacts left in the remains of Tenochtitlán to learn more about the Aztecs and their life in the city.

GLOSSARY

canal: a man-made waterway

civilization: an organized society with written records and laws

conquistador: a Spanish conqueror or adventurer

culture: the beliefs and ways of life of a group of people

curfew: a time someone must be home by

descendant: a person who comes after another in a family

nomad: a person who wanders from place to place to find shelter and food

sacrifice: the act of killing as an offering to please a god

society: the people who live together in an organized community with traditions, laws, and values

translator: someone who tells what words in one language mean in another

vision: something seen by a way other than normal sight, such as in sleep or the imagination

worship: to honor as a god

FOR MORE INFORMATION

BOOKS

Cooke, Tim. *The Aztecs.* Mankato, MN: Brown Bear Books, 2015.

MacDonald, Fiona. *You Wouldn't Want to Be an Aztec Sacrifice!: Gruesome Things You'd Rather Not Know.* New York, NY: Franklin Watts, 2014.

WEBSITES

Aztec Facts for Kids

www.dkfindout.com/us/history/aztecs/

This website gives interesting information about the Aztec people and their culture.

History for Kids: Aztecs, Maya, and Inca

www.ducksters.com/history/aztec_maya_inca.php

Read more about three of the oldest civilizations of the Americas here.

INDEX